America As A Case Study In The Harmful Effects of Religion

By Max Humana

America As A Case Study In The Harmful Effects of Religion. 1st Edition

Published by Reality Publishing, LLC. Copyright © 2018, Reality Publishing, LLC. Content is taken from the book *Thank god For Eve,* copyright © 2018, published in 2019.

All Rights Reserved.

For more information, contact Reality Publishing, LLC at realitypublishing2100@gmail.com.

Copyright infringement is against the law. If you believe the copy of this book you are reading infringes on the author's copyright, please notify the publisher at realitypublishing2100@gmail.com.

No part of this book may be reproduced, stored in a retrieval system or transmitted in any form or by any means, electronic, mechanical, photocopying, recording or otherwise, except for brief quotations, without express written permission of the publisher.

Cover design by Max Humana.

Cover photograph of storm clouds in South Dakota taken by Don Whitebread, courtesy NOAA's National Weather Service (NWS) Collection, NOAA Weather in Focus Photo Contest 2015.

Cover image of the United States is a Landsat image of the continental United States merged with terrain. Courtesy U.S. Geological Survey, Department of the Interior / USGS.

ISBN: 978-1-7332857-0-4

Other Books By The Author

Thank god For Eve; Why Religion Exists And Why It Must Go

An Opening Salvo On Coexistence; Plus Everybody's An Atheist And I Can Prove It (Chapter Eleven from the book *Thank god For Eve* as a separate pamphlet)

Thou Shalt Not Think; How Psychology Subverts Reason And Opens Pandora's Box of Faith (Chapter Twelve from the book *Thank god For Eve* as a separate pamphlet)

Religions Are Fruitful, They Multiply, And They Are Very Bad For You (Chapter Fifteen from the book *Thank god For Eve* as a separate pamphlet)

Why Is Any Moral Person Still A Catholic? (The Church of Evil, Abnormality and Hypocrisy) (Chapter Twenty-One from the book *Thank god For Eve* as a separate pamphlet)

America's Completely Secular Founding Documents (More Christian Attempts At Rewriting History) (Chapter Twenty-Seven from the book *Thank god For Eve* as a separate pamphlet)

Religious Freedom Laws, Also Known As "My god Says You're A Piece of Shit" (Chapter Twenty-Eight from the book *Thank god For Eve* as a separate pamphlet)

Four Degrees of Separation

Dedication

This book is dedicated to all brave, courageous and happily godless freethinkers, humanists, secularists, scientists and supporters of science and reason in all times and in all places.

It is dedicated to every person who has ever advanced the causes of science and reason at the expense of dogma. All these wonderful fellow humans deserve heartfelt credit and our collective thanks for their expansion of human knowledge.

From the first evidence-minded freethinking *Homo heidelbergensis* who raised a furry skeptical eyebrow at his fellow troopmate's obeisance to an imaginary entity, to our likeminded godless kin in the far distant future who will quite likely have to continue today's fight to keep religion and state safely separate, I salute you all.

Your courage in standing up for reason in the face of persecution and ignorance, your battles against mindless tradition and those who believe their god is on their side, and your never-ending pursuit of a better life for all creatures on this planet all demonstrate that imaginary gods only get in the way of doing what is right and what is good.

Religion's long war on reason and the reasonable has left long trails of tears and blood across our world. The image below depicts the kind of Inquisitional treatment which the deeply and sincerely faithful have so frequently and so eagerly inflicted upon fellow human beings who chose to think for themselves.

Spanish Inquisition.

The faithful have tortured and killed more people, and damaged more minds, bodies and lives, than we will ever be able to count. I would be inconceivably remiss if I did not sincerely dedicate this book to all of the men, women, children and the unborn who have lost their freedom and their lives at the willing hands of the devout.

Contents

Acknowledgments

America As A Case Study In The Harmful Effects of Religion   1

About The Author   31

References   33

Acknowledgments

All humans owe their very existence to their ancestors, and this existence is made flesh in the form of our bodies and brains. Our interactions with our parents, families and societies strongly shape our attitudes and perceptions. Thus in the true spirit of genesis, I must first and foremost thank my parents for passing on to me the blend of genes which made me an empiricist and a realist. Fortunately, my inherited DNA orients me away from fear, superstition and its unjustified dogmas and toward courage, reason and an empirical reality.

I must also thank them, and primarily my mother, for providing an environment conducive to learning, thinking and advancement in the pursuit of education and intellectual self-development. The exclusion from our home of any requirements for dogmatic thinking and blind obedience to authority, combined with the freedom we had to explore ideas and information as a pure and unconstrained pursuit, set the conditions for many years of delightful reading, talking and thinking.

I also cannot thank my mother enough for the numerous instances of her selfless parenthood which I witnessed from my earliest years on this planet. My memories of these acts will remain with me until my very last conscious moment. Without ever calling attention to them, she set the example of what it means to actually do things for other people without any expectation of reciprocation, recognition or reward. My mother was also instrumental in keeping me in the best schools she could find even when we could not afford them, and has been focused on education and critical thinking for as long as I can remember. I owe her, quite literally, everything I am, and I will always be grateful for it.

I must also thank my wife for her endless patience as I perused references, pored over transcripts, pounded away at the keyboard and spent time in dialogue with the faithful. And most of all, I want to thank her for her love and companionship.

America As A Case Study In The Harmful Effects of Religion

"The various modes of worship, which prevailed in the Roman world, were all considered by the people, as equally true; by the philosopher, as equally false; and by the magistrate, as equally useful."
- Edward Gibbon

"Religion is an insult to human dignity. Without it you would have good people doing good things and evil people doing evil things. But for good people to do evil things, that takes religion."
- Steven Weinberg

Religion has been a debilitating and deadly cancer on humanity since it was first invented, and it has metastasized and spread into every nation and society on earth. It has no real answers to anything, but it pretends it has information of ultimate truth and value delivered from the great beyond. It has been the cause of untold amounts of pain and misery deliberately inflicted on innocent bodies and minds.

It is pitiless and unflinching in its faith-based proclamations, pogroms and persecutions. It spares no one, from helpless small children to elderly men and women and from devout fundamentalists to the wholly secular who must continually battle its attacks on humanity, reason and indeed on the secular themselves.

It aggressively fights against science and reason and when it cannot kill, burn or deny the facts or their discoverers, it twists the new facts to fit ancient desert fairy tales written by astoundingly ignorant and hateful people. It tries to make its fiction the law of the land and thuggishly tries to force its holy books and their immoralities down everyone else's throats.

That it has been able to do all this for thousands of years without a scrap of actual evidence or justification for its actions is a sad testimony to the many weaknesses of the human mind and the dogged persistence of human ignorance, stupidity and evil.

Far from being either true or helpful, religion is merely astrology on steroids, alchemy claiming divine writ and human ignorance codified in highly immoral and thoroughly corrupt human tribal institutions.

All of the thousands of humanity's invented religions contradict each other, and the schisms within these religions number in the tens of thousands. They cannot all be right, yet this does not stop them all from claiming to have the one true hotline to heaven.

Religions offer us gods to worship who are allegedly all-loving but who are quite happy to kill individual people, whole cities or even every life form on the entire planet, including large numbers of children both born and unborn, in psychopathic fits of rage.

It is impossible to count up all the bodies and minds which have been damaged or destroyed by religion and its practitioners, but the tally continues to skyrocket faster than the American national debt, even as science continues to make discoveries that religion has never, could never and will never make.

Religion makes people dumb and immoral, and it makes societies and nations dumb and immoral. Any system of thought that turns to ignorance as its first problem-solving option is intellectually and morally bankrupt and will always generate far more human misery than human well-being.

Religion is a mind-numbing, critical thinking-killing mental opiate which is antithetical to a truly humanistic society, and it is high time we all grow up and live in the real world without the self-imposed cancer of religion.

The brief history of the United States is a microcosm of the long battle between ignorance and enlightenment. The timeline of religious history in the US a few paragraphs below is a listing of significant events in American history which shows how religion captures vulnerable minds, justifies extreme immorality and the infliction of suffering, and fights the advance of science and reason with everything it has.

This includes deliberately lying to whoever it needs to lie to, and lying however it needs to, in order to achieve its end goal of religious power and supremacy.

For its entire history, religion's motto has been that the end justifies the means. For the deeply and sincerely faithful believer and the religious zealot, it cannot be said often enough that when a person believes his god is on his side, nothing is sacred. In the eyes of the faithful, no lie is too big, no deception is too immoral and no campaign of misinformation is too inappropriate, because they believe they are doing their god's will.

Facts do not matter to the faithful, and they never will. Religion is not a fact-based belief system; it is a belief-based belief system. It is a self-reinforcing mental cocoon which is constructed to prevent undesired facts from entering. Evidence is extremely unwelcome in religion, because reality contradicts the faith. And in what may be the ultimate perversity and malfunction of the human brain, the harder one pushes facts at the believer, the more tightly he closes his mind to them.

Every human alive needs to understand this, most especially the secular, the rational and the well-educated, because these people think that all one need do to make a person stop believing in his faith and doing insane things in its service is to provide him with sufficient facts and evidence against the faith.

This will not work, because, again, facts do not matter in religion and they never will. In order to properly combat this institutionalized and aggressive ignorance, the secular and the truly rational among us need to understand this. We must also understand the fight against ignorance will be a long and bitter one.

Perhaps in several thousand years, if human evolution moves along the path of increasing receptivity to facts and decreasing susceptibility to fear and emotion, all humans will one day actually use facts instead of feelings as justification for their most important decisions and beliefs. But this will not be the case for the rest of this millennium and almost certainly for at least a handful of millennia after that.

Until one day in the far distant future when humans have matured as a species and religion finally dies off, it will do all it can to keep its chokehold on humanity. It will continue to deny facts. The faithful will continue to say and do immoral things and continue to try to maintain power over real people in the real world. The timeline below of just a few events in the continual counterpunching by the warring parties of enlightenment and religious immorality and ignorance in America illustrates this quite clearly.

1620[1]   The Pilgrims arrive in Massachusetts after fleeing religious strife and persecution in Europe, intent on keeping their tribal and cultural identity.

1650-1815[2] The European Enlightenment enabled critical thinking, reason and humanism to flourish and to show the errors and immorality of religion and a better path to human well-being. Enlightenment ideas strongly affected the American Founding Fathers and shaped America's founding documents.

1692[3]   The Salem, Massachusetts witch trials, a series of religiously-motivated trials of more than 200 people accused of being witches, led to 20 executions and many people being jailed.

1730-1755[4] The "First Great Awakening" was the first in a series of zealous and often evangelical and fundamentalist Christian revivals in America.

1776[5]   Signing of the US Declaration of Independence, a wholly secular and Enlightenment-informed document.

Part Six of *Thank god For Eve* contains much more on the subject of our godless founding documents and godless founding national ethos, which contradicts today's religious falsehoods claiming otherwise.

1789[6] — Institution of the fully secular US Constitution, prepared by Enlightenment thinkers.

1790-1840[7] — The "Second Great Awakening" was another religious revival, this one in response to the secularism and deism of the Enlightenment and the belief that the Second Coming was near. This never-occurring but always-promised Second Coming is a recurring theme.

1791[8] — The First Amendment to the Constitution was enacted, quite intelligently preventing government establishment of religion.

1797[9] — The US signed a formal treaty with Tripoli which specifically states the US is "…not in any sense founded on the Christian Religion…" Thus from 1776 to 1797 both major national founding documents and a treaty with a foreign nation, all approved by top government leadership, show the US government and founding ethos to be wholly secular.

1800-1850[10] — The general period of the "Burned Over District", which was an area of west and central New York which experienced a series of religious crazes which ignited then quickly burned out, and which was fertile ground for much of the Second Great Awakening's fads. Such religious cycling was not unusual in the rest of the country and shows the extreme human gullibility and susceptibility to religion without the need for actual evidence.

This was the modern-day equivalent of the ancient Mediterranean hotbed of religions, in which religions and gods were continually invented, traded and cross-bred, and which eventually produced Judaism, Christianity and Islam.

1813-present[11]   Christian Dispensationalism, a fundamentalist sect in which the faithful believe their god has divided history into specific time periods and humanity is responsible for "stewardship".

1826[12]   Joseph Smith, the founder of Mormonism, experiences his first legal conviction. This one was for being "a disorderly person and an imposter". Smith was from New York, home of the aforementioned religion-addled Burned Over District.

1830[13]   Joseph Smith founds Mormonism in western New York, based on his claim of being able to translate magical gold

	plates by using magic stones and a hat. Despite the rest of its teachings being just as crazy and fact-free, Mormonism is still going strong today.
1831[14]	William Miller founds the Millerite sect, which believed the Second Coming would happen before 1843. Miller is also from New York, continuing the trend of new and wholly evidence-free religious fads and sects forming in that area.
1844[15]	The "Great Disappointment" in the Millerite movement was the feeling these people expressed in October 1844 when Miller's prophesied date for the Second Coming came and went without Jesus making an appearance or even sending an RSVP.
1848-1920[16]	Spiritualism, a belief that the living can communicate with the dead, is popular with millions of Americans. It, too, arose in religion-addled New York, fully devoid of evidence.
1855-1930[17]	The "Third Great Awakening" was another time of religious fervor, fundamentalism, zealotry and great concern about the often-promised but never actually occurring Second Coming.
1861[18]	The American Civil War is fought largely because the strongly Christian

	southern states refused to give up their biblically-justified slavery. Well over 600,000 Americans died in this utterly avoidable faith-based war.
1863[19]	The Seventh-day Adventist Church, a fundamentalist spinoff sect of the now-defunct Millerites, is formed. It is also extremely anxious about the long-awaited Second Coming.
1865[20]	The 13th Amendment made slavery illegal in America, thus going against the Christian bible's support of slavery. Despite the country being overwhelmingly populated by Christians who proclaimed their religion as moral, it took all the way to 1865 to do away with this evil practice. The deeply devout Christians of the American South made the lives of former slaves extremely miserable for many years afterward, and still today work to block their descendants from voting. If Christianity were truly moral even to the tiniest degree, there would never have been a slave trade or this continuing deliberate evil.
1866-present[21]	The Ku Klux Klan is formed after the criminalization of slavery and remains active today as a white Christian supremacist organization.

1870[22] The 15th Amendment enacted voting rights for nonwhites and former slaves. This anti-biblical granting of human rights and equality faced significant opposition, in a country that was almost exclusively self-professedly moral and Christian.

1873[23] Congress passed the religiously motivated Comstock Act, which actually made it a crime to have or have information about medications or methods for contraception or so-called "unlawful" abortion. Some states passed laws far harsher than the federal act, and actually made married couples subject to imprisonment for using birth control *in their own homes*.

Some Comstock language remained on the books until parts were removed in 1971 and others astoundingly into the 1990s. This is theocracy, and it is what always happens when the church is allowed to intrude into the state. The faithful go very far out of their way to legislate their personal religion and jam it down everyone else's throats.

1877-1964[24] The overwhelmingly Christian South had segregationist Jim Crow laws on the books for almost a hundred years. Black Americans had to live in so-called "separate but equal" conditions in some of the most devout states in America, and lived with reduced well-being in every aspect of life. Again, the allegedly moral followers of Christianity didn't merely fail to correct this travesty, they kept it going for as long as possible.

1896[25]   The Supreme Court, in the case of *Plessy v Ferguson*, decided by a seven to one vote that the "separate but equal" conditions were legal and thus enabled legal segregation and oppression of black Americans for many years afterward. Meaning that solely due to the color of a person's skin, Christian America felt it perfectly fine to forbid certain people from certain locations or facilities. Jesus's "do unto others" was wholly ignored.

1916[26]   Margaret Sanger is arrested after opening the first birth control clinic in the US.

1918-1920[27]   Approximately 675,000 Americans died in the 1918 Spanish Flu pandemic, despite trillions of prayers offered to Jesus and his father for deliverance from the plague.

1920-1933[28]   Religious zealots in the US, led by the Woman's Christian Temperance Union, convinced Congress to enact Prohibition via the 18th Amendment. Alcohol was largely banned in the country at various levels and in various jurisdictions but of course religious use of wine got an undeserved exception. The faithful continued their efforts to try to order other people around, using the legal system to thuggishly force their personal faith on other people whenever they could. This cycle never ends.

1920[29]   In an overwhelmingly Christian America, and after a very long struggle against much strong opposition, it took until 1920 to enact the 19th Amendment which also anti-biblically gave women the right to vote. The fights against segregation and for equal treatment of black and female Americans had to be waged against entrenched Christian opposition, since their bible specifically supports slavery and puts women under male control. By comparison, New Zealand's women could vote in 1893.

1925[30]   After Darwin's scientifically true theory of evolution made its way into American schools, religious fundamentalists and zealots fought extremely hard to remove it. Tennessee passed the infamous Butler Act which actually blocked public school teachers from teaching evolution and denying biblical creation. Again, the faithful imposed their unjustified beliefs on others through the corruption of the legal system. Based on the politics in that state and in many other places in the US today, nothing has changed.

1925[31]	John Scopes, a substitute teacher in Tennessee, was prosecuted in what is called the Scopes Monkey Trial for violating the Butler Act. During the trial, the prosecution thoroughly embarrassed itself by its blatant denial of science and reason and its abject adherence to the fictional stories and dogmas in the Christian bible. The religious again show their zeal to suppress real science and teach fact-free dogma.
1925-1927[32]	Mississippi and Arkansas enact Butler Act-like anti-evolution laws. Again, nothing has changed in 100 years as these states are still contaminated by religion, and science-denying religion has now infected government and politics at the national level.
1942-present[33]	Christian Nationalism began in America and is still extant today.
1945+[34]	Due to the religious suppression of science, technology, engineering and math (STEM) in US schools, and the impacts on education in the 1930s due to the Great Depression, major droughts and the Dust Bowl, all of which occurred despite trillions of heartfelt prayers to Jesus, the US needed to bring Werner von Braun and over a thousand other scientists to the country after World War II to work on rocketry and other programs.

1947-1958[35] The US endured McCarthyism, the modern day equivalent of witch trials but without the hangings and burnings, along with the Red Scare, an existential fear of the Soviet Union. The US began its retreat into a cocoon of religion due to fears over war with the so-called "godless communist" Russia.

1950-1958[36] Religiosity was extremely high in America; largely a rebound effect after WWII and due to anticommunism, McCarthyism and the Red Scare. American schools were not rigorous and STEM training in particular was not strong. Schools were racially segregated during this strongly religious period despite the *Brown vs Board of Education* Supreme Court decision in 1954. American Christians, as they still do today, hypocritically wanted equality and fair treatment to mean that they got to make the rules which everybody else had to follow, thus segregation and religiosity were both entrenched.

1952[37] The science fiction writer L. Ron Hubbard invents Scientology. The insanity of its teachings and beliefs exceed even those of Mormonism and the three Mesopotamian monotheisms, as one would expect from a science fiction writer.

1954[38] The Supreme Court unanimously decides in the *Brown vs Board of*

Education case that the 1896 *Plessy vs Ferguson* decision was wrong and that segregation in schools was unconstitutional. Finally we have an actual moral decision made by the highest court in a highly religious but legally secular nation. The decision was nevertheless highly unpopular with much of Christian America.

1954[39] Rising religious zealotry led to "under god" being added to the Pledge of Allegiance. This wholly unnecessary act was both unconstitutional and a symptom of the country's increasing religious fundamentalism. It was another example of the Christian faithful working very hard to impose their personal opinions onto American life and politics.

1954-1968[40] The American civil rights movement took a very long time to reach major milestones, and again in a majority Christian nation the lack of those Christians doing much for and often fighting against the civil rights of their fellow citizens is a damning condemnation of their morality and their religion.

1956-1975[41] The Space Race between the US and the Soviet Union sets the backdrop for some of the developments in America over the next decade.

1956[42]	The out of control national religious fervor and the continuing attempts by the Christian faithful to inculcate and infiltrate the government led to the replacement of the national motto with "In God We Trust". It had been "E Pluribus Unum" since 1782.

Christian aggression and powerlust led the country to throw out almost two hundred years of an excellent and fully inclusive motto in favor of a sop to Christianity. The Christian god had never done a single damn thing to deserve any trust, but this did not stop the faithful. |
| 1956[43] | For the faithful, changing the national motto wasn't enough unconstitutional interference by religion in state matters so "In God We Trust" was put on US paper currency. This was to be the last major act of empty-headed and religiously driven buffoonery for some time, thanks to what the Russians did in the following year. |
| 1957[44] | The Soviet Union launched the first artificial satellite, Sputnik 1. This act of technological overmatch by a looming enemy badly shocked and scared the US. National leaders took a hard and honest look at the poor quality of STEM education and training in the US. |

1958[45]	In response to Sputnik and the perceived existential danger of Soviet technological overmatch, the Eisenhower Administration implemented many science initiatives to get America's religiously drugged heads out of the clouds and focused on STEM. This included creating DARPA and NASA and passing the National Defense Education Act, intended to get US schools out of the faith-induced pits they were in.

1960[46]	Ruby Bridges was the first black child to attend an all-white elementary school in the South. Yes, it took all the way to 1960 in devout Christian America for this to happen.

1960-1980[47]	The "Fourth Great Awakening" was the last spike in Christian fundamentalism, and it differed from the previous episodes in that more fundamentalist groups like Southern Baptists gained size and power. They also faced a growing secular and humanistic opposition, which had not previously been the case.

This opposition meant, in clear Darwinian terms, that the more aggressive and fundamentalist religious species would thrive. This is what happened then and it is what is still happening today in both American religion and politics as the more fervent and active strains of the religious virus continue to infect citizens and governments.

1963[48] George Wallace, the new Alabama governor, called for "segregation now, segregation tomorrow, segregation forever", and later in the year actually stood in front of a door at the University of Alabama to try to physically stop black students from entering. The federalized Alabama National Guard had to tell him to get out of the way.

Alabama's Christians voted in a poisonous hateful segregationist and bigot as their governor, on purpose, not just once but *four* separate times. It took an unsuccessful assassination attempt to make Wallace finally see the light of empathy. If the shooting was Wallace's Damascus Road experience, the Christian god utterly failed to intervene at the right time.

1965[49] President Lyndon Johnson signed the Voting Rights Act which prohibited discrimination and other practices intended to suppress the votes of black and other minority Americans. Religious fundamentalists, bigots and thugs are nevertheless still working hard even unto this day to suppress minority votes all across America.

1965-present[50] Christian Reconstructionism and Dominion theology are active in America. They seek to transform the US into a Christian-dominated country under biblical laws. The only word for what this would be is horrifying, as such a state would be as cruel and unjust as the modern Islamic State or the medieval Catholic State under the popes.

1968[51] Martin Luther King, Jr. is shot and killed in Memphis, Tennessee. He was only one of many civil rights activists and leaders who were murdered because they wanted equal rights for fellow human beings in Christian America and wouldn't stop fighting for them.

1968[52] The Supreme Court ruled in *Epperson vs Arkansas* that an Arkansas law preventing the teaching of human evolution in public schools was unconstitutional. Like the *Brown vs Board of Education* case, reason and sanity began to guide some of these SCOTUS decisions. The faithful did not let this defeat stop them, of course. They decided that since science and the Constitution were now at long last being used by the courts to decide cases, they had to repackage their fundamentalism and creationism into a form that sounded scientific.

Thus, and again in an ironically classic Darwinian selection process, they created a body of fact-free dogmatic nonsense called "creation science" and tried to inject this into public school instruction. Some areas actually enacted legislation requiring that this Frankenstein be taught in schools along with evolution.

1982[53] The US District Court for the Eastern District of Arkansas ruled that the Arkansas law requiring public schools to teach "creation science" was unconstitutional. The judge in the case was very precise in defining science and why "creation science" most certainly was not science but was just religious dogma.

Fundamentalists and creationists across the US saw this latest defeat of their newest Trojan Horse and began working on a newer strain which they hoped would successfully infect the public school system.

1987[54] The SCOTUS ruled in *Edwards v. Aguillard* that a Louisiana law mandating "creation science" be taught along with evolution was also unconstitutional and that the law was intended to support a specific religion. The scientific community, including 72 science Nobel Prize winners, was engaged. Numerous entities filed amicus briefs to inform the court on the scientific truth of the matter and the utter religiosity of "creation science".

1989[55] Following these defeats in the courts of law and common sense, the fundamentalist and creationist community invents so-called "Intelligent Design Creationism" as the latest strain of religious virus, designed and built specifically to sound scientific enough to pass Establishment Clause muster. Not to *be* scientific enough, just to *sound* that way.

Religious zealots and fundamentalists continue their efforts to inject this newest Trojan Horse virus into public school biology classes. This would lead to the famous 2005 showdown in Dover, Pennsylvania, noted below.

2000[56] First election of George W. Bush, a strongly conservative, born-again, antiscientific Republican Christian who expressly, gratuitously and unconstitutionally catered to the religious right. Science not supporting Christianity or Republican goals was suppressed. He either then or later believed he was chosen by his god to be president and to do his god's bidding. He let religion infest the White House and it greatly affected foreign and domestic policy, particularly foreign

	policy following the attacks on September 11, 2001.
2003[57]	George W. Bush and Tony Blair, two religiously blinded and dogmatic theocrats, invade Iraq on bad information, false pretenses and a belief that their god had placed them in office to spread the word of that god and do his bidding on earth. Again, Christians continually show their inability to think clearly. Bush and Blair were merely modern-day Crusaders doing the work the old popes didn't complete, and Bush unbelievably actually used the word "crusade" until someone gave him a basic history lesson and told him that was a breathtakingly stupid choice of words.
2004[58]	Second election of George W. Bush. Things got far worse as time went on. Religion continued to have a special place and special protection. Science was under constant attack during the entire period of Bush's time in office, by people motivated by religion, ignorance, science denial and greed.
2005[59]	In a perfect example of the totality of the fight between reason and ignorance, the latest Christian Trojan Horse of so-called Intelligent Design Creationism and the façade of Christian honesty and morality were mercilessly exposed and viciously eviscerated in the *Kitzmiller v.*

Dover Area School District case. This case exposed both the lie of ID and the lies of the faithful who pushed it on the people. So-called "creation science" had been a loser in court, so the Dover, Pennsylvania school district had mandated in 2004 that ID be taught. Intelligent and Constitutionally correct parents sued to stop it.

Every person who uses reason should read the full accounts of the case, both to understand the slimy deceitful depths to which the faithful will sink in service of their god and its dogma, and to be prepared for the next mutation of the creationist virus when it infects another school district. The judge in the case, a Republican and George W. Bush appointee, deserves massive amounts of respect and credit for the way he objectively applied science, facts, reason and the law to the case and his ruling.

2008[60] First election of Barack Obama, a progressive, half-black, freethinking and moral intellectual who quite professionally and Constitutionally, and unlike so many of his predecessors, never let the church into state matters. He also was the first US president to mention nonbelievers as part of the national family.

He restored science to its rightful place as the arbiter of truth and reason, and made immense strides in restoring the nation's focus on science and moral issues such as health care and income inequality. He was fought tooth and nail on each of these issues by entrenched Christian and Christian Republican opposition.

2012[61] Second election of Obama. He continues to fight for science and human rights and is vigorously opposed at every turn by dogmatic and science-denying Christians. These Christians have turned their Jesus into a war-mongering, firearm-loving bigot and spend endless hours and dollars spreading that message.

2012[62] The Texas Republican party's official platform states its formal opposition to critical thinking with these words, which need to live in disgusting infamy: "We oppose the teaching of Higher Order Thinking Skills (HOTS) (values clarification), critical thinking skills and similar programs that are simply a relabeling of Outcome-Based Education (OBE) (mastery learning) which focus on behavior modification and have the purpose of challenging the student's fixed beliefs and undermining parental authority."

There it is, in their own words. Christian Republicans oppose critical thinking and the challenging of fixed beliefs, no matter how wrong they may be, if they challenge uninformed beliefs and authority. This is the religion-driven authoritarianism and totalitarianism which true morality, science and reason are always fighting against.

2016[63] Evangelicals and many other Christians hypocritically vote overwhelmingly for Donald Trump in the US presidential election, despite his blatant and repeated public violations of every biblical commandment they supposedly hold dear. Again, as in their entire history, and as they will act whenever they can get away with it, the religious act according to their motto "the end justifies the means", and they will elect literally anyone who will enforce their immoral religion on other people.

This administration's war on science and reason is a full-out blitzkrieg, starting with a Pearl Harbor-like attack followed by unceasing actions to demolish rational and science-based institutions and research and install science-denying dogmatic satraps into cabinet and other positions. Science, truth and reason become systematically "unpersoned", as data vanish from websites and scientists are muzzled or fired for contradicting the Pravda.

Additionally, not only is Russia now a highly aggressive destroyer of stability and American integrity, the US government now openly caters to one of our country's primary adversaries like a blushing teenage girl with a crush. Far from the Red Scare of the 1950s, today's Republicans, evangelicals and many Christians are displaying earth-shattering levels of intentional cuckoldry by openly letting the barbarian enemies at the gate gain dangerous access and influence while deliberately tearing down their own castle ramparts and defenses.

2018[64]   In a blatantly pandering move intended to stroke Christians and their tremendously fragile egos, the Trump administration moved the US embassy in Israel to Jerusalem.

The record is crystal clear and the pattern is unchanging. Religion and its adherents are a clear and present danger to the well-being, safety and security of individuals and societies, and the short history of America is a textbook example of the damage religion does. To the faithful, no lie is too big to tell in the service of the mission to make every other person bend the knee and live under a theocratic government and its biblical laws.

The Christian faithful in America never cease their hypocritical and immoral campaign of propaganda and subversion, seeking to impose their particular god and their particular religion on everyone else, and they never stop lying about it.

The attempts by Christians to force then to sneak religion into America's secular public schools show a clear pattern of Darwinian evolution. When they could no longer mandate religion in the schools, they tried different ways to portray religion as science. Since this is impossible, those attempts failed and they are now back to the drawing board trying to figure out their next attack. I predict their next salvo will be less of a direct attack on science and the Constitution than an even more underhanded attack, and one that uses the progressive ideals of equality and inclusion against themselves.

This is actually being done now, as the faithful prattle on and on about their freedom of religion while they use that freedom to justify their oppression and bigotry. I predict they will see that trying to force religion into science or to make them compatible is a nonstarter, at least until they can pack the courts with enough judges who will deny the words of the Constitution in service of dogma, so they will try to use other areas of education, such as sociology or philosophy or some other line of thought.

They will probably not seek in the near term to directly inject their god, as that kind of subversion would be immediately detected and Constitutionally beaten back for the Nth time, but they will seek to inject their version of morality and their teachings though a back door, under the banner of "multiculturalism" and "exposure to other perspectives". When challenged, they will scream that "the (liberals / progressives / scientists / leftists) are discriminating against us! All we want to do is expose the children to more points of view!"

Whenever any of you liberals, progressives, scientists and most importantly, educators, hear this, as you inevitably will, you need to suppress your initial reaction to give in to your "multicultural" or "fairness" instincts, you need to grab that lying BS out of the air before it hurts someone and use it to verbally beat the liar who said it within an inch of his lying life.

These people put on the "I'm a nice Christian" front but it is a deliberate lie and a deliberate deception, just like most everything else they do. Theirs is a Crusade which never ends. They don't play fair and they will manipulate words, laws and people to get what they want. You must aggressively and unceasingly stop, block and prevent any of this nonsensical garbage from polluting our schools. We can't stop these people from polluting their own families and their own children at home, but we damn sure can stop them from forcing it into the schools.

To paraphrase Winston Churchill when the armies of darkness were attacking his great nation, we shall fight to the end, we shall fight them in the halls, we shall fight on the courtyards and public squares, we shall fight with growing certainty and growing strength in the courts, we shall defend our schools, whatever the cost may be. We shall expose them in the media, we shall fight in the school districts, we shall fight in the towns and in the streets, we shall fight in state capitols; we shall never surrender!

Religion has made America very dumb over and over again, and each time it is beaten back it returns in mutated form ready for another attack on science, reason and morality. Today as we struggle to put our military back together after a 15-year-long modern crusade that has accomplished absolutely nothing except killing and injuring far too many of our own and other people and doing grave damage to the US Treasury and our national morality, we find ourselves in a very bad position.

As we emerged from the small and dark Middle Eastern cave where we have been fighting, blinking under the blazing sun as we move on to the much larger global field of gladiatorial combat, we have taken a good look at our adversaries and realized that our former superiority in science and technology is a thing of the past.

We fought a very long crusade for very wrong reasons, "led" by a religiously blinded theocrat, and now we find ourselves struggling in almost every area to prepare our armed forces for an actual major war which will combine virtual, economic and physical weapons.

While our blood and treasure fought this faith-based war in a religion-addled region of the world, in far too many cases returning with badly damaged minds and bodies or in coffins, our elected theocratic science deniers and unelected religious thugs fought with everything they had to deny and suppress science, dumb down education and make their religious dogma the law of the land.

The faithful have done everything they can to enact modern-day Butler and Comstock Acts, they have put prohibitions on critical thinking and actual science, and they have set the conditions for another and much more destructive Sputnik Moment. And they are doing it on purpose, in the open, without shame, and with the full complicity of far too many Americans whose sons and daughters will be the ones who will needlessly die in the next Hot War.

We are already beginning to be overcome by our many adversaries' advances in the battlefields of the classroom, the laboratory and the marketplace. We cannot let the faithful drag us down past the point of no return in these battlefields as they have already come close to doing in the traditional field of battle.

We are on the cusp of such a global and permanent shift in national power and station. Unless we want to become just another theocracy, banana republic or fascist state, we must regain our sanity and strongly and completely reject the antiscientific, the anti-intellectual, and the extremely harmful dogmas of the ignorant and the faithful. If we do not, the next "Sputnik Moment" may be the death knell of our great nation and our grand experiment.

About The Author

Max Humana is a retired US military servicemember who still supports and defends the Constitution against all enemies both foreign and domestic through writing on the never-safe subjects of religion, politics, morality, humanity, truth and reason.

He is working to advance human knowledge and to rid the world of ignorance, stupidity and evil, and wants you to do the same.

References

1. Smithsonian.com article on *"Pilgrims' Progress"*. Web resource at https://www.smithsonianmag.com/history/pilgrims-progress-135067108/
2. Web resource at https://www.britannica.com/event/Enlightenment-European-history
3. Web resource at https://www.britannica.com/event/Salem-witch-trials
4. Web resource at https://en.wikipedia.org/wiki/First_Great_Awakening
5. Transcript of the Declaration of Independence. Web resource at https://www.archives.gov/founding-docs/declaration-transcript
6. Transcript of the US Constitution. Web resource at https://www.archives.gov/founding-docs/constitution-transcript
7. Web resource at https://en.wikipedia.org/wiki/Second_Great_Awakening
8. Constitution of the United States. Web resource at https://www.senate.gov/civics/constitution_item/constitution.htm
9. Yale Law School Avalon Project, *"The Barbary Treaties 1786-1816; Treaty of Peace and Friendship, Signed at Tripoli November 4, 1796"*. Web resource at http://avalon.law.yale.edu/18th_century/bar1796t.asp
10. Web resource at https://en.wikipedia.org/wiki/Burned-over_district
11. Web resource at https://en.wikipedia.org/wiki/Dispensationalism

12. Web resource at https://en.wikipedia.org/wiki/Joseph_Smith_and_the_criminal_justice_system
13. Web resource at https://en.wikipedia.org/wiki/Mormonism
14. Web resource at https://en.wikipedia.org/wiki/Millerism
15. Web resource at https://en.wikipedia.org/wiki/Great_Disappointment
16. Web resource at https://en.wikipedia.org/wiki/Spiritualism
17. Web resource at https://en.wikipedia.org/wiki/Third_Great_Awakening
18. National Park Service information on casualties in the Civil War. Web resource at https://www.nps.gov/nr/travel/national_cemeteries/death.html
19. Web resource at https://en.wikipedia.org/wiki/Seventh-day_Adventist_Church
20. The 13th Amendment to the U.S. Constitution: Abolition of Slavery. Web resource at https://www.ourdocuments.gov/doc.php?flash=false&doc=40
21. Article on the Ku Klux Klan. Web resource at http://www.pbs.org/wgbh/americanexperience/features/klansville-faq/
22. The Constitution of the United States. Web resource at https://www.senate.gov/civics/constitution_item/constitution.htm
23. Web resource at https://www.britannica.com/event/Comstock-Act
24. Web resource at https://www.britannica.com/event/Jim-Crow-law

25. Cornell Law School's Legal Information Institute information on the 1896 Plessy v. Ferguson Supreme Court case. Web resource at https://www.law.cornell.edu/supremecourt/text/163/537
26. Public Broadcasting Service information on Margaret Sanger. Web resource at https://www.pbs.org/wgbh/americanexperience/features/pill-margaret-sanger-1879-1966/
27. Centers for Disease Control and prevention information on the 1918 flu pandemic. Web resource at https://www.cdc.gov/features/1918-flu-pandemic/index.html
28. Public Broadcasting Service information on Prohibition. Web resource at http://www.pbs.org/kenburns/prohibition/
29. The Constitution of the United States. Web resource at https://www.senate.gov/civics/constitution_item/constitution.htm
30. National Center for Science Education information on the Butler Act; site shows the Butler act in image form. Web resource at https://ncse.com/files/pub/legal/Scopes/Butler_Act.pdf
31. Web resource at https://www.britannica.com/event/Scopes-Trial
32. Article titled *"The Ban on the Teaching of Evolution Reaches the U.S. Supreme Court"*, the third in a series on "Creationism in the United States". Article written by Randy Moore, found in *The American Biology Teacher*, Volume 60, No. 9, November/December 1998. Web resource at Mississippi and Arkansas enact Butler Act-like anti-evolution laws

33. Web resource at https://en.wikipedia.org/wiki/Christian_nationalism - United_States
34. Web resource at https://en.wikipedia.org/wiki/Operation_Paperclip
35. Article from the University of Virginia's Miller Center titled *"McCarthyism and the Red Scare"*. Web resource at https://millercenter.org/the-presidency/educational-resources/age-of-eisenhower/mcarthyism-red-scare
36. University of Southern California article titled *"The 1950s – Powerful Years for Religion"*, written by Carol Tucker, dated June 16, 1997. Web resource at https://news.usc.edu/25835/The-1950s-Powerful-Years-for-Religion/
37. Web resource at https://en.wikipedia.org/wiki/Scientology
38. Cornell Law School's Legal Information Institute information on the 1654 Brown v. Board of Education Supreme Court case. Web resource at https://www.law.cornell.edu/supremecourt/text/347/483
39. Web resource at https://www.britannica.com/event/Pledge-of-Allegiance-to-the-Flag-of-the-United-States-of-America
40. Web resource at https://en.wikipedia.org/wiki/Timeline_of_the_civil_rights_movement
41. Article on Smithsonian.com titled *"The Space Race"*, written by Michael Kernan for Smithsonian Magazine, dated August 1997. Web resource at https://www.smithsonianmag.com/history/the-space-race-141404095/
42. Web resource at https://en.wikipedia.org/wiki/In_God_We_Trust

43. Web resource at https://en.wikipedia.org/wiki/In_God_We_Trust
44. Article on NASA.gov titled "*Sputnik and The Dawn of the Space Age*", updated October 10, 2007 by Steve Garber, NASA History Web Curator. Web resource at https://history.nasa.gov/sputnik/
45. Web resource at https://en.wikipedia.org/wiki/Sputnik_1
46. Web resource at https://en.wikipedia.org/wiki/Timeline_of_the_civil_rights_movement
47. Web resource at https://en.wikipedia.org/wiki/Fourth_Great_Awakening
48. Web resource at https://en.wikipedia.org/wiki/Timeline_of_the_civil_rights_movement
49. Web resource at https://en.wikipedia.org/wiki/Timeline_of_the_civil_rights_movement
50. Web resource at https://en.wikipedia.org/wiki/Christian_reconstructionism
51. Web resource at https://en.wikipedia.org/wiki/Timeline_of_the_civil_rights_movement
52. Web resource at https://en.wikipedia.org/wiki/Epperson_v._Arkansas
53. Web resource at https://en.wikipedia.org/wiki/McLean_v._Arkansas
54. Cornell Law School's Legal Information Institute information on the 1987 Edwards v. Aguillard Supreme Court case. Web resource at https://www.law.cornell.edu/supremecourt/text/482/578

55. University of California, Berkeley article titled *"Intelligent Design: Is it scientific?"* Web resource at https://undsci.berkeley.edu/article/id_checklist
56. Article in *The Nation* online magazine, titled *"Bush's War on Science"*, written by Katrina vanden Heuvel, dated July 20, 2004. Web resource at https://www.thenation.com/article/bushs-war-science/
57. Council on Foreign Relations article, titled *"The Iraq Invasion Ten Years Later: A Wrong War"*, an interview. Interviewer Bernard Gwertzman, interviewee Richard N. Haass, dated March 13, 2013. Web resource at https://www.cfr.org/interview/iraq-invasion-ten-years-later-wrong-war
58. Article in *MIT Technology Review* online, titled *"The Anti-Science President"*, by David Ewing Duncan, dated July 12, 2007. Web resource at https://www.technologyreview.com/s/408236/the-anti-science-president/
59. National Center for Science Education article titled *"Kitzmiller v. Dover: Intelligent Design on Trial"*. Web resource at https://ncse.com/library-resource/kitzmiller-v-dover-intelligent-design-trial
60. White House statement titled *"IMPACT REPORT: 100 Examples of President Obama's Leadership in Science, Technology, and Innovation"*, from the Office of the Press Secretary, dated June 21, 2016. Web resource at https://obamawhitehouse.archives.gov/the-press-office/2016/06/21/impact-report-100-examples-president-obamas-leadership-science
61. Article in *The Scientist*, titled *"TS Picks: Obama's Science Legacy"*, by Joshua A. Krisch, dated January 17, 2017. Web resource at https://www.the-

scientist.com/the-nutshell/ts-picks-obamas-science-legacy-32194
62. The 2012 Republican Party of Texas Report of Platform Committee and Rules Committee. Web resource at https://www.empowertexans.com/wp-content/uploads/2012/07/2012-GOP-Platform-Final.pdf
63. Article in *Scientific American* titled "*The Trump Administration's War on Science Agencies Threatens the Nation's Health and Safe*ty", by Andrew A. Rosenberg and Kathleen Rest, dated January 1, 2018. Web resource at https://www.scientificamerican.com/article/the-trump-administration-rsquo-s-war-on-science-agencies-threatens-the-nation-rsquo-s-health-and-safety/
64. British Broadcasting Corporation article titled "*Jerusalem embassy: Why Trump's move was not about peace*", by Barbara Plett Usher, dated May 15, 2018. Web resource at https://www.bbc.com/news/world-us-canada-44120428

Made in the USA
Columbia, SC
02 May 2025